THE SEASONS OF LOVE

EXTRACTS FROM
THE PLAYS AND POEMS
OF
WILLIAM SHAKESPEARE

OSBORNE
HERITAGE

Published by Osborne Books Limited
Unit 1b Everoak Estate, Bromyard Road,
Worcester, WR2 5HN
General Editor: Michael Fardon
Cover Design: Louise Ferebee, Pineapple Publishing
Printed by the Bath Press, Bath

ISBN 1 872962 56 4

Contents

Introduction

The Tudor and Stuart age produced some of the finest love lyrics of all time. In this volume we present extracts from the poems and plays of William Shakespeare.

The book is divided into the four seasons because the passage of love follows in its many stages the progress of the year. Springtime sees the birth of love with all its hopes, Summer brings heat and passion, Autumn mellow warmth and maturity. Winter finally closes in as the deserted and desolate lover waits for the new Spring.

Readers should note that the titles given to the poems in this book are not the original titles, but are presented here to encapsulate the mood of each passage. A commentary has also been added to explain each extract.

part the first

Spring

Hark, hark, the lark

Hark, hark, the lark at heaven's gate sings,
   And Phoebus gins arise,
His steeds to water at those springs
   On chaliced flowers that lies;
And winking Mary-buds begin
   To ope their golden eyes.
With every thing that pretty is,
   My lady sweet, arise,
      Arise, arise!

from 'Cymbeline'

A song of sunrise and the awakening of the beloved lady.

It was a lover and his lass

It was a lover and his lass,
    With a hey, and a ho, and a hey nonino,
That o'er the green cornfield did pass
    In springtime, the only pretty ringtime,
When birds do sing, hey ding a ding, ding.
Sweet lovers love the spring.

Between the acres of the rye,
    With a hey, and a ho, and a hey nonino,
These pretty country folks would lie
    In springtime, the only pretty ringtime,
When birds do sing, be ding a ding, ding.
Sweet lovers love the spring.

This carol they began that hour,
    With a hey, and a ho, and a hey nonino,
How that a life was but a flower
    In springtime, the only pretty ringtime,
When birds do sing, hey ding a ding, ding.
Sweet lovers love the spring.

And therefore take the present time,

    With a hey, and a ho, and a hey nonino,

For love is crowned with the prime

    In springtime, the only pretty ringtime,

When birds do sing, hey ding a ding, ding.

Sweet lovers love the spring.

from 'As You Like It'

A springtime song of rural love ~ take pleasure at the 'present time' ~ while it lasts.

4

'Come kiss me, sweet and twenty'

What is love? 'Tis not hereafter;
Present mirth hath present laughter;
    What's to come is still unsure:
In delay there lies no plenty;
Then come kiss me, sweet and twenty,
    Youth's a stuff will not endure.

from 'Twelfth Night'

A song sung by Feste to Sir Toby Belch and Sir Andrew Aguecheek.

5

Lovesick Romeo

But soft! What light through yonder window breaks?
It is the East, and Juliet is the sun!
Arise, fair sun, and kill the envious moon,
Who is already sick and pale with grief
That thou her maid art far more fair than she.
Be not her maid, since she is envious.
Her vestal livery is but sick and green,
And none but fools do wear it. Cast it off.
It is my lady; O, it is my love!
O that she knew she were!
She speaks, yet she says nothing. What of that?
Her eye discourses; I will answer it.

See how she leans her cheek upon her hand!
O that I were a glove upon that hand,
That I might touch that cheek!

from 'Romeo and Juliet'

Romeo swoons at the sight of Juliet appearing at her balcony.

Come, Romeo; come

Come, night; come, Romeo; come, thou day in night;
For thou wilt lie upon the wings of night
Whiter than new snow upon a raven's back.
Come, gentle night; come, loving, black-browed night;
Give me my Romeo; and, when he shall die,
Take him and cut him out in little stars,
And he will make the face of heaven so fine
That all the world will be in love with night
And pay no worship to the garish sun.
O, I have bought the mansion of a love,
But not possessed it, and though I am sold,
Not yet enjoyed. So tedious is this day
As is the night before some festival
To an impatient child that hath new robes
And may not wear them.

from 'Romeo and Juliet'

Juliet longs for her wedding night.

7

Who is Silvia?

Who is Silvia? What is she,
    That all our swains commend her?
Holy, fair, and wise is she;
    The heaven such grace did lend her,
That she might admired be.

Is she kind as she is fair?
    For beauty lives with kindness.
Love doth to her eyes repair,
    To help him of his blindness,
And, being helped, inhabits there.

Then to Silvia let us sing,
    That Silvia is excelling.
She excels each mortal thing
    Upon the dull earth dwelling.
To her let us garlands bring.

from 'Two Gentlemen of Verona'

One gentleman woos another gentleman's lady!

8

O happy breeze!

On a day (alack the day!)
Love, whose month is ever May,
Spied a bosom passing fair
Playing in the wanton air.
Through the velvet leaves the wind,
All unseen, can passage find;
That the lover, sick to death,
Wished himself the heaven's breath.
Air, quoth he, thy cheeks may blow;
Air, would I might triumph so,
But, alack, my hand is sworn
Ne'er to pluck thee from thy thorn.

from 'Love's Labours Lost'

Dumaine reads out his passionate writings.

9

His lover's face

So sweet a kiss the golden sun gives not
   To those fresh morning drops upon the rose,
As thy eye-beams when their fresh rays have
smote
   The night of dew that on my cheeks down
flows.
Nor shines the silver moon one half so bright
   Through the transparent bosom of the deep
As doth thy face, through tears of mine, give
light.

from 'Love's Labours Lost'

The King of Navarre reads out his passionate writings.

10

All your acts are queens

                                    What you do
Still betters what is done. When you speak, sweet,
I'd have you do it ever. When you sing,
I'd have you buy and sell so, so give alms,
Pray so, and for the ord'ring your affairs,
To sing them too. When you do dance, I wish you
A wave o' th' sea, that you might ever do
Nothing but that, move still, still so,
And own no other function. Each your doing,
So singular in each particular,
Crowns what you are doing in the present deeds,
That all your acts are queens.

from 'The Winter's Tale'

*Prince Florizel pours out his love to Perdita, a princess
disguised as a shepherdess.*

Nature falls a-doting

A woman's face, with Nature's own hand painted,
Hast thou, the master-mistress of my passion;
A woman's gentle heart, but not acquainted
With shifting change, as is false women's fashion;
An eye more bright than theirs, less false in rolling,
Gilding the object whereupon it gazeth;
A man in hue all hues in his controlling,
Which steals men's eyes and women's souls amazeth.
And for a woman wert thou first created,
Till Nature as she wrought thee fell a-doting,
And by addition me of thee defeated
By adding one thing to my purpose nothing.
 But since she pricked thee out for women's pleasure,
 Mine be thy love, and thy love's use their treasure.

Sonnet 20

Nature herself falls in love, but is the object of desire a man or a woman?

My love is as fair . . .

So is it not with me as with that Muse
Stirred by a painted beauty to his verse,
Who heaven itself for ornament doth use
And every fair with his fair doth rehearse;
Making a couplement of proud compare
With sun and moon, with earth and sea's rich gems,
With April's first-born flowers, and all things rare
That heaven's air in this huge rondure hems.
O let me, true in love, but truly write,
And then believe me, my love is as fair
As any mother's child, though not so bright
As those gold candles fixed in heaven's air:
    Let them say more that like of hearsay well;
    I will not praise that purpose not to sell.

Sonnet 21

True love does not flatter, but writes 'truly.'

He dares not speak his love

As an unperfect actor on the stage,
Who with his fear is put besides his part,
Or some fierce thing replete with too much rage,
Whose strength's abundance weakens his own heart;
So I, for fear of trust, forget to say
The perfect ceremony of love's rite,
And in mine own love's strength seem to decay,
O'ercharged with burden of mine own love's might.
O, let my books be then the eloquence
And dumb presagers of my speaking breast,
Who plead for love, and look for recompense,
More than that tongue that hath more expressed.
    O, learn to read what silent love hath writ:
    To hear with eyes belongs to love's fine wit.

Sonnet 23

*The poet is too overwhelmed to speak his love, and uses his pen
to express his feelings.*

14

The beloved outshines Spring

What is your substance, whereof are you made,
That millions of strange shadows on you tend?
Since every one hath, every one, one shade,
And you, but one, can every shadow lend.
Describe Adonis, and the counterfeit
Is poorly imitated after you.
On Helen's cheek all art of beauty set,
And you in Grecian tires are painted new.
Speak of the spring and foison of the year:
The one doth shadow of your beauty show,
The other as your bounty doth appear,
And you in every blessed shape we know.
    In all external grace you have some part,
    But you like none, none you, for constant heart.

Sonnet 53

The lover waxes lyrical about the beauty of the beloved.

15

Venus woos Adonis

These extracts from the extended poem 'Venus and Adonis' tell how Venus, the Goddess of Love, seduces the beautiful and innocent youth Adonis while he is out hunting.

Even as the sun with purple-colored face
Had ta'en his last leave of the weeping morn,
Rose-cheeked Adonis hied him to the chase.
Hunting he loved, but love he laughed to scorn.
 Sick-thoughted Venus makes amain unto him
 And like a bold-faced suitor 'gins to woo him.

'Thrice fairer than myself,' thus she began,
'The field's chief flower, sweet above compare,
Stain to all nymphs, more lovely than a man,
More white and red than doves or roses are,
 Nature that made thee, with herself at strife,
 Saith that the world hath ending with thy life.

'Vouchsafe, thou wonder, to alight thy steed,
And rein his proud head to the saddlebow.
If thou wilt deign this favor, for my meed
A thousand honey secrets shalt thou know.
   Here come and sit, where never serpent hisses
   And being set, I'll smother thee with kisses.

'Touch but my lips with those fair lips of thine
Though mine be not so fair, yet are they red
The kiss shall be thine own as well as mine.
What seest thou in the ground? Hold up thy head.
   Look in mine eyeballs, there thy beauty lies,
   Then why not lips on lips, since eyes in eyes?

'Art thou ashamed to kiss? Then wink again,
And I will wink so shall the day seem night.
Love keps his revels where there are but twain.
Be bold to play; our sport is not in sight.
   These blue-veined violets whereon we lean
   Never can blab, nor know not what we mean.

17

'Thou canst not see one wrinkle in my brow;
Mine eyes are grey and bright and quick in turning;
My beauty as the spring doth yearly grow,
My flesh is soft and plump, my marrow burning;
    My smooth moist hand, were it with thy hand felt,
    Would in thy palm dissolve or seem to melt.

Sometime she shakes her head, and then his hand;
Now gazeth she on him, now on the ground;
Sometime her arms infold him like a band ~
She would, he will not in her arms be bound;
    And when from thence he struggles to be gone;
    She locks her lily fingers one in one.

'Fondling,' she saith, 'since I have hemmed thee here
Within the circuit of this ivory pale,
I'll be a park, and thou shalt be my deer:
Feed where thou wilt, on mountain or in dale;
    Graze on my lips; and if those hills be dry,
    Stray lower, where the pleasant fountains lie.

18

'Within this limit is relief enough,
Sweet bottom-grass, and high delightful plain,
Round rising hillocks, brakes obscure and rough,
To shelter thee from tempest and from rain.
    Then be my deer, since I am such a park;
    No dog shall rouse thee, though a thousand bark.'

Now let me say "Good night," and so say you.
If you will say so, you shall have a kiss.'
'Good night,' quoth she; and, ere he says 'Adieu,'
The honey fee of parting tend'red is:
    Her arms do lend his neck a sweet embrace;
    Incorporate then they seem; face grows to face;

Till breathless he disjoined, and backward drew
The heavenly moisture, that sweet coral mouth,
Whose precious taste her thirsty lips well knew,
Whereon they surfeit, yet complain on drouth.
    He with her plenty pressed, she faint with dearth,
    Their lips together glued, fall to the earth.

Now quick desire hath caught the yielding prey,
And glutton-like she feeds, yet never filleth.
Her lips are conquerors, his lips obey,
Paying what ransom the insulter willeth;
    Whose vulture thought doth pitch the price so high
    That she will draw his lips' rich treasure dry.

Hot, faint, and weary with her hard embracing,
Like a wild bird being tamed with too much handling,
Or as the fleet-foot roe that's tired with chasing,
Or like the froward infant stilled with dandling,
    He now obeys and now no more resisteth,
    While she takes all she can, not all she listeth.

When he did frown, O, has she then gave over,
Such nectar from his lips she had not sucked.
Foul words and frowns must not repel a lover.
What though the rose have prickles, yet tis plucked.
    Were beauty under twenty locks kept fast,
    Yet love breaks through and picks them all at last.

 20

part the second

Summer

Shall I compare thee to a summer's day?

Shall I compare thee to a summer's day?
Thou art more lovely and more temperate.
Rough winds do shake the darling buds of May,
And summer's lease hath all too short a date.
Sometime too hot the eye of heaven shines,
And often is his gold complexion dimmed;
And every fair from fair sometime declines,
By chance, or nature's changing course, untrimmed:
But thy eternal summer shall not fade
Nor lose possession of that fair thou ow'st,
Nor shall Death brag thou wand'rest in his shade
When in eternal lines to time thou grow'st.
    So long as men can breathe or eyes can see,
    So long lives this, and this gives life to thee.

Sonnet 18

A passionate outpouring to the beloved whose beauty is compared to an 'eternal summer' which 'shall not fade.'

Eternity was in our lips and eyes

Eternity was in our lips and eyes,
Bliss in our brows' bent: none our parts so poor
But was a race of heaven.

from 'Antbony and Cleopatra'

Cleopatra sees their love as literally 'heavenly.'

Visions of Anthony

Where think'st thou be is now? Stands be, or sits be?
Or does be walk? or is be on bis borse?
O happy borse, to bear the weight of Antony!
Do bravely, borse! for wot'st thou whom thou mov'st?
The demi-Atlas of this earth, the arm
And burgonet of men. He's speaking now,
Or murmuring, 'Where's my serpent of old Nile?'
(For so be calls me). Now I feed myself
With most delicious poison. Think on me,
That am with Phoebus' amorous pinches black
And wrinkled deep in time!

from 'Anthony and Cleopatra'

The obsessed Cleopatra muses on the absent Anthony.

All-consuming Cleopatra

Age cannot wither her, nor custom stale
Her infinite variety: other women cloy
The appetites they feed, but she makes hungry
Where most she satisfies.

from 'Anthony and Cleopatra'

Anthony recognises that their love is all-consuming.

Love's night-time journey

Weary with toil, I haste me to my bed,
The dear repose for limbs with travail tired,
But then begins a journey in my head
To work my mind when body's work's expired;
For then my thoughts, from far where I abide,
Intend a zealous pilgrimage to thee,
And keep my drooping eyelids open wide,
Looking on darkness which the blind do see;
Save that my soul's imaginary sight
Presents thy shadow to my sightless view,
Which, like a jewel hung in ghastly night,
Makes black night beauteous and her old face new,
  Lo, thus, by day my limbs, by night my mind,
  For thee and for myself no quiet find.

Sonnet 27

*The lover, weary with thinking about love during the day, is
kept awake at night by a vision of the beloved, a 'jewel in
ghastly night.'*

What is wealth?

When, in disgrace with Fortune and men's eyes,
I all alone beweep my outcast state,
And trouble deaf heaven with my bootless cries,
And look upon myself and curse my fate,
Wishing me like to one more rich in hope,
Featured like him, like him with friends possessed,
Desiring this man's art, and that man's scope,
With what I most enjoy contented least;
Yet in these thoughts myself almost despising,
Haply I think on thee, and then my state,
Like to the lark at break of day arising
From sullen earth, sings hymns at heaven's gate;
  For thy sweet love rememb'red such wealth brings
  That then I scorn to change my state with kings.

Sonnet 29

*The lover forgets his envy of other men's wealth at the
thought of his 'sweet love.'*

Take all my loves, my love

Take all my loves, my love, yea, take them all:
What hast thou then more than thou hadst before?
No love, my love, that thou mayst true love call;
All mine was thine before thou hadst this more.
Then, if for my love thou my love receivest,
I cannot blame thee for my love thou usest;
But yet be blamed if thou this self deceivest
By wilful taste of what thyself refusest.
I do forgive thy robb'ry, gentle thief,
Although thou steal thee all my poverty;
And yet love knows it is a greater grief
To bear love's wrong than hate's known injury.
  Lascivious grace, in whom all ill well shows,
  Kill me with spites; yet we must not be foes.

Sonnet 40

The lover asks how he can give more when his beloved already has his heart.

When dreams do show thee me

When most I wink, then do mine eyes best see,
For all the day they view things unrespected;
But when I sleep, in dreams they look on thee
And, darkly bright, are bright in dark directed.
Then thou, whose shadow shadows doth make bright,
How would thy shadow's form form happy show
To the clear day with thy much clearer light
When to unseeing eyes thy shade shines so!
How would, I say, mine eyes be blessed made
By looking on thee in the living day,
When in dead night thy fair imperfect shade
Through heavy sleep on sightless eyes doth stay!
  All days are nights to see till I see thee,
   And nights bright days when dreams do show thee me.

Sonnet 43

The lover contemplates the perfection of his beloved seen through the eyes of sleep.

Sweet rose

O, how much more doth beauty beauteous seem
By that sweet ornament which truth doth give:
The rose looks fair, but fairer we it deem
For that sweet odor which doth in it live.
The canker blooms have full as deep a dye
As the perfumed tincture of the roses,
Hang on such thorns, and play as wantonly
When summer's breath their masked buds discloses;
But, for their virtue only is their show,
They live unwooed and unrespected fade,
Die to themselves. Sweet roses do not so:
Of their sweet deaths are sweetest odors made.
    And so of you, beauteous and lovely youth,
    When that shall fade, my verse distills your truth.

Sonnet 54

The poet knows that rose blooms will eventually die, but he is able to preserve the heady beauty of their scent in his poetry.

Sweet love, renew thy force

Sweet love, renew thy force; be it not said
Thy edge should blunter be than appetite,
Which but to-day by feeding is allayed,
To-morrow sharp'ned in his former might.
So, love, be thou: although to-day thou fill
Thy hungry eyes even till they wink with fulness,
To-morrow see again, and do not kill
The spirit of love with a perpetual dulness.
Let this sad int'rim like the ocean be
Which parts the shore where two contracted new
Come daily to the banks, that, when they see
Return of love, more blest may be the view;
   Or call it winter, which, being full of care,
   Makes summer's welcome thrice more wished, more rare.

Sonnet 56

*The lover, anxious that too much love will dull his appetite, asks
that each new day will dawn like the coming of summer.*

31

The blind slavery of love

Being your slave, what should I do but tend
Upon the hours and times of your desire?
I have no precious time at all to spend,
Nor services to do till you require.
Nor dare I chide the world-without-end hour
Whilst I, my sovereign, watch the clock for you,
Nor think the bitterness of absence sour
When you have bid your servant once adieu.
Nor dare I question with my jealous thought
Where you may be, or your affairs suppose,
But, like a sad slave, stay and think of nought
Save where you are how happy you make those.
   So true a fool is love that in your will,
   Though you do anything, he thinks no ill.

Sonnet 57

*The lover is such a 'sad slave' to passion that every hour of
the day is devoted to the beloved – whether present or absent.*

Love alters not

Let me not to the marriage of true minds
Admit impediments; love is not love
Which alters when it alteration finds
Or bends with the remover to remove.
O, no, it is an ever-fixed mark
That looks on tempests and is never shaken;
It is the star to every wand'ring bark,
Whose worth's unknown, although his height be taken.
Love's not Time's fool, though rosy lips and cheeks
Within his bending sickle's compass come;
Love alters not with his brief hours and weeks,
But bears it out even to the edge of doom.
  If this be error, and upon me proved,
  I never writ, nor no man ever loved.

Sonnet 116

The poet confidently asserts that true love 'alters not' and is
'never shaken.'

No false comparisons

My mistress' eyes are nothing like the sun;
Coral is far more red than her lips' red;
If snow be white, why then her breasts are dun;
If hairs be wires, black wires grow on her head.
I have seen roses damasked, red and white,
But no such roses see I in her cheeks;
And in some perfumes is there more delight
Than in the breath that from my mistress reeks.
I love to hear her speak; yet well I know
That music hath a far more pleasing sound:
I grant I never saw a goddess go;
My mistress, when she walks, treads on the ground.
  And yet, by heaven, I think my love as rare
    As any she belied with false compare.

Sonnet 130

The poet flouts convention and abandons the traditional
flattery of the beloved.

part the third

Autumn

Take, O take those lips away

Take, O take those lips away,
  That so sweetly were forsworn;
And those eyes, the break of day,
  Lights that do mislead the morn;
But my kisses bring again, bring again,
Seals of love, but sealed in vain, sealed in vain.

from 'Measure for Measure'

A boy sings to Mariana who has been rejected by her lover.

When thou shalt scarcely greet me

Against that time, if ever that time come,
When I shall see thee frown on my defects,
Whenas thy love hath cast his utmost sum,
Called to that audit by advised respects;
Against that time when thou shalt strangely pass
And scarcely greet me with that sun, thine eye,
When love, converted from the thing it was,
Shall reasons find of settled gravity:
Against that time do I ensconce me here
Within the knowledge of mine own desert,
And this my hand against myself uprear
To guard the lawful reasons on thy part.
   To leave poor me thou has the strength of laws,
   Since why to love I can allege no cause.

Sonnet 49

*The lover prepares himself for the time when he is no longer
loved and when the beloved will 'scarcely greet' him.*

Time doth transfix

Like as the waves make towards the pebbled shore,
So do our minutes hasten to their end;
Each changing place with that which goes before,
In sequent toil all forwards do contend.
Nativity, once in the main of light,
Crawls to maturity, wherewith being crowned,
Crooked eclipses 'gainst his glory fight,
And Time that gave doth now his gift confound.
Time doth transfix the flourish set on youth
And delves the parallels in beauty's brow,
Feeds on the rarities of nature's truth,
And nothing stands but for his scythe to mow:
   And yet to times in hope my verse shall stand,
   Praising thy worth, despite his cruel hand.

Sonnet 60

*The poet muses on the march of time and the process of
ageing but knows that his verse will remain immortal.*

Age's cruel knife

Against my love shall be as I am now,
With Time's injurious hand crushed and o'erworn;
When hours have drained his blood and filled his brow
With lines and wrinkles, when his youthful morn
Hath travelled on to age's steepy night,
And all those beauties whereof now he's king
Are vanishing, or vanished out of sight,
Stealing away the treasure of his spring ~
For such a time do I now fortify
Against confounding age's cruel knife,
That he shall never cut from memory
My sweet love's beauty, though my lover's life.
  His beauty shall in these black lines be seen,
   And they shall live, and be in them still green.

Sonnet 63

*The poet consoles himself that his verse will preserve his
beloved against the 'cruel knife' ~ the ravages of time.*

The decay of time

Since brass, nor stone, nor earth, nor boundless sea,
But sad mortality o'ersways their power,
How with this rage shall beauty hold a plea,
Whose action is no stronger than a flower?
O, how shall summer's honey breath hold out
Against the wrackful siege of batt'ring days,
When rocks impregnable are not so stout,
Nor gates of steel so strong but Time decays?
O fearful meditation: where, alack,
Shall Time's best jewel from Time's chest lie hid?
Or what strong hand can hold his swift foot back,
Or who his spoil of beauty can forbid?
    O, none, unless this miracle have might,
    That in black ink my love may still shine bright.

Sonnet 65

*The poet takes consolation that his verse – his 'black ink' – will
resist Time's 'swift foot' and keep his love shining bright.*

No longer mourn for me

No longer mourn for me when I am dead
Than you shall hear the surly sullen bell
Give warning to the world that I am fled
From this vile world, with vilest worms to dwell.
Nay, if you read this line, remember not
The hand that writ it, for I love you so
That I in your sweet thoughts would be forgot
If thinking on me then should make you woe.
O, if, I say, you look upon this verse
When I, perhaps, compounded am with clay,
Do not so much as my poor name rehearse,
But let your love even with my life decay,
   Lest the wise world should look into your moan
   And mock you with me after I am gone.

Sonnet 71

*The poet muses on his death and hopes that the sorrow of his
beloved after his death will decay as his body will.*

Only a dream

Farewell: thou art too dear for my possessing,
And like enough thou know'st thy estimate.
The charter of thy worth gives thee releasing;
My bonds in thee are all determinate.
For how do I hold thee but by thy granting,
And for that riches where is my deserving?
The cause of this fair gift in me is wanting,
And so my patent back again is swerving.
Thyself thou gav'st, thy own worth then not knowing,
Or me, to whom thou gav'st it, else mistaking;
So thy great gift, upon misprision growing,
Comes home again, on better judgment making.
　　Thus have I had thee as a dream doth flatter,
　　In sleep a king, but waking no such matter.

Sonnet 87

The poet asleep is a 'king' in love, but awakes to find he is not worthy of the beloved.

42

The passing of beauty's summer

To me, fair friend, you never can be old,
For as you were when first your eye I eyed,
Such seems your beauty still. Three winters cold
Have from the forests shook three summers' pride,
Three beauteous springs to yellow autumn turned
In process of the seasons have I seen,
Three April perfumes in three hot Junes burned,
Since first I saw you fresh, which yet are green.
Ah, yet doth beauty, like a dial hand,
Steal from his figure, and no pace perceived;
So your sweet hue, which methinks still doth stand,
Hath motion, and mine eye may be deceived;
    For fear of which, hear this, thou age unbred:
    Ere you were born was beauty's summer dead.

Sonnet 104

*The poet sees the contradiction in the fact that the beloved
still has beauty but beauty is always passing with time.*

Leaving the home of love

O, never say that I was false of heart,
Though absence seemed my flame to qualify;
As easy might I from myself depart
As from my soul, which in thy breast doth lie.
That is my home of love: if I have ranged,
Like him that travels I return again,
Just to the time, not with the time exchanged,
So that myself bring water for my stain.
Never believe, though in my nature reigned
All frailties that besiege all kinds of blood,
That it could so preposterously be stained
To leave for nothing all thy sum of good;
   For nothing this wide universe I call
   Save thou, my rose; in it thou art my all.

Sonnet 109

The poet contemplates returning to his beloved, his 'rose', his 'all.'

44

Confessions of betrayal

Alas, 'tis true I have gone here and there
And made myself a motley to the view,
Gored mine own thoughts, sold cheap what is most dear,
Made old offences of affections new.
Most true it is that I have looked on truth
Askance and strangely; but, by all above,
These blenches gave my heart another youth,
And worse essays proved thee my best of love.
Now all is done, have what shall have no end:
Mine appetite I never more will grind
On newer proof, to try an older friend,
A god in love, to whom I am confined.
　　Then give me welcome, next my heaven the best,
　　Even to thy pure and most loving breast.

Sonnet 110

The poet confesses that he has cheapened his love by being
unfaithful but wishes to return to the beloved's 'pure breast.'

Thou blind fool, Love

Thou blind fool, Love, what dost thou to mine eyes
That they behold and see not what they see?
They know what beauty is, see where it lies,
Yet what the best is take the worst to be.
If eyes, corrupt by over-partial looks,
Be anchored in the bay where all men ride,
Why of eyes' falsehood has thou forged hooks,
Whereto the judgment of my heart is tied?
Why should my heart think that a several plot
Which my heart knows the wide world's common place?
Or mine eyes seeing this, say this is not,
To put fair truth upon so foul a face?
   In things right true my heart and eyes have erred,
   And to this false plague are they now transferred.

Sonnet 137

*The poet complains that Love – a 'blind fool' – is distorting his
perceptions and clouding his judgement.*

Love's false flattery

When my love swears that she is made of truth
I do believe her, though I know she lies,
That she might think me some untutored youth,
Unlearned in the world's false subtilties.
Thus vainly thinking that she thinks me young,
Although she knows my days are past the best,
Simply I credit her false-speaking tongue:
On both sides thus is simple truth suppressed.
But wherefore says she not she is unjust?
And wherefore say not I that I am old?
O, love's best habit is in seeming trust,
And age in love loves not to have years told.
   Therefore I lie with her and she with me,
    And in our faults by lies we flattered be.

Sonnet 138

*The poet acknowledges that he and his beloved are happy to
accept the fact that they conceal the truth from each other.*

My love is as a fever

My love is as a fever, longing still
For that which longer nurseth the disease,
Feeding on that which doth preserve the ill,
Th' uncertain sickly appetite to please.
My reason, the physician to my love,
Angry that his prescriptions are not kept,
Hath left me, and I desperate now approve
Desire is death, which physic did except.
Past cure I am, now reason is past care,
And frantic-mad with evermore unrest;
My thoughts and my discourse as madmen's are,
At random from the truth vainly expressed:
   For I have sworn thee fair, and thought thee bright,
   Who art as black as hell, as dark as night.

Sonnet 147

The poet is suffering from the self-destructive fever of love;
reason has left him 'frantic-mad with evermore unrest.'

48

part the fourth

Winter

Come away, come away, death

Come away, come away, death,
    And in sad cypress let me be laid.
Fie away, fie away, breath;
    I am slain by a fair cruel maid.
My shroud of white, stuck all with yew,
    O, prepare it.
My part of death, no one so true
    Did share it.

Not a flower, not a flower sweet,
    On my black coffin let there be strown;
Not a friend, not a friend greet
    My poor corpse, where my bones shall be
thrown
A thousand thousand sighs to save,
    Lay me, O, where
Sad true lover never find my grave,
    To weep there.

Song from 'Twelfth Night'

 50

Consolation for the broken heart?

Why didst thou promise such a beauteous day
And make me travel forth without my cloak,
To let base clouds o'ertake me in my way,
Hiding thy brav'ry in their rotten smoke?
'Tis not enough that through the cloud thou break
To dry the rain on my storm-beaten face,
For no man well of such a salve can speak
That heals the wound, and cures not the disgrace:
Nor can thy shame give physic to my grief;
Though thou repent, yet I have still the loss:
Th' offender's sorrow lends but weak relief
To him that bears the strong offence's cross.
   Ah, but those tears are pearl which thy love sheds,
   And they are rich and ransom all ill deeds.

Sonnet 34

*A brief ray of sunshine gives temporary consolation to the
broken-hearted lover.*

Loss in love

That thou hast her, it is not all my grief,
And yet it may be said I loved her dearly;
That she hath thee is of my wailing chief,
A loss in love that touches me more nearly.
Loving offenders, thus I will excuse ye:
Thou dost love her because thou know'st I love her,
And for my sake even so doth she abuse me,
Suff'ring my friend for my sake to approve her.
If I lose thee, my loss is my love's gain,
And losing her, my friend hath found that loss:
Both find each other, and I lose both twain,
And both for my sake lay on me this cross.
    But here's the joy: my friend and I are one;
    Sweet flattery! then she loves but me alone.

Sonnet 42

*The lover loses his beloved to his friend, and in so doing, loses
both, except that . . .*

My grief lies onward

How heavy do I journey on the way
When what I seek (my weary travel's end)
Doth teach that ease and that repose to say,
'Thus far the miles are measured from thy friend.'
The beast that bears me, tired with my woe,
Plods dully on, to bear that weight in me,
As if by some instinct the wretch did know
His rider loved not speed, being made from thee.
The bloody spur cannot provoke him on
That sometimes anger thrusts into his hide,
Which heavily he answers with a groan,
More sharp to me than spurring to his side;
  For that same groan doth put this in my mind:
  My grief lies onward and my joy behind.

Sonnet 50

The grief-stricken lover reluctantly journeys away from his beloved, leaving his 'joy behind.'

Alone in the weary night

Is it thy will thy image should keep open
My heavy eyelids to the weary night?
Dost thou desire my slumbers should be broken
While shadows like to thee do mock my sight?
Is it thy spirit that thou send'st from thee
So far from home into my deeds to pry,
To find out shames and idle hours in me,
The scope and tenure of thy jealousy?
O no, thy love, though much, is not so great;
It is my love that keeps mine eye awake,
Mine own true love that doth my rest defeat
To play the watchman ever for thy sake.
  For thee watch I whilst thou dost wake elsewhere,
  From me far off, with others all too near.

Sonnet 61

*The poet lies awake at night, alone, and thinking of his beloved
who seems so distant both in body and in affections.*

54

The time of yellow leaves

That time of year thou mayst in me behold
When yellow leaves, or none, or few, do hang
Upon those boughs which shake against the cold,
Bare ruined choirs where late the sweet birds sang.
In me thou seest the twilight of such day
As after sunset fadeth in the west,
Which by and by black night doth take away,
Death's second self that seals up all in rest.
In me thou seest the glowing of such fire
That on the ashes of his youth doth lie,
As the deathbed whereon it must expire,
Consumed with that which it was nourished by.
   This thou perceiv'st, which makes thy love more strong,
    To love that well which thou must leave ere long.

Sonnet 73

The poet muses on the irony that the fires of love still burn
in the twilight of life and now consume him on his 'deathbed.'

Then hate me now

Then hate me when thou wilt, if ever, now;
Now, while the world is bent my deeds to cross,
Join with the spite of fortune, make me bow,
And do not drop in for an after-loss.
Ah, do not, when my heart hath scaped this sorrow,
Come in the rearward of a conquered woe;
Give not a windy night a rainy morrow,
To linger out a purposed overthrow.
If thou wilt leave me, do not leave me last,
When other petty griefs have done their spite,
But in the onset come: so shall I taste
At first the very worst of fortune's might;
  And other strains of woe, which now seem woe,
  Compared with loss of thee will not seem so.

Sonnet 90

The poet, in despair, begs his beloved to spurn him now so that his greatest sorrow can also be the most immediate.

How like a winter hath my absence been

How like a winter hath my absence been
From thee, the pleasure of the fleeting year!
What freezings have I felt, what dark days seen,
What old December's bareness everywhere!
And yet this time removed was summer's time,
The teeming autumn, big with rich increase,
Bearing the wanton burden of the prime,
Like widowed wombs after their lords' decease:
Yet this abundant issue seemed to me
But hope of orphans and unfathered fruit;
For summer and his pleasures wait on thee,
And, thou away, the very birds are mute;
    Or, if they sing, 'tis with so dull a cheer
    That leaves look pale, dreading the winter's near.

Sonnet 97

The poet compares his absence from his beloved to the cheerless winter.

57

Yet seemed it winter

From you have I been absent in the spring,
When proud-pied April, dressed in all his trim,
Hath put a spirit of youth in everything,
That heavy Saturn laughed and leapt with him;
Yet nor the lays of birds, nor the sweet smell
Of different flowers in odor and in hue,
Could make me any summer's story tell,
Or from their proud lap pluck them where they grew:
Nor did I wonder at the lily's white,
Nor praise the deep vermilion in the rose;
They were but sweet, but figures of delight,
Drawn after you, you pattern of all those.
   Yet seemed it winter still, and you away,
   As with your shadow I with these did play.

Sonnet 98

The joys that Spring and Summer bring seem like Winter in
the absence of the beloved.

58

Be wise as thou art cruel

Be wise as thou art cruel: do not press
My tongue-tied patience with too much disdain,
Lest sorrow lend me words, and words express
The manner of my pity-wanting pain.
If I might teach thee wit, better it were,
Though not to love, yet, love, to tell me so;
As testy sick men, when their deaths be near,
No news but health from their physicians know.
For if I should despair, I should grow mad,
And in my madness might speak ill of thee:
Now this ill-wresting world is grown so bad
Mad slanderers by mad ears believed be.

   That I may not be so, nor thou belied,
   Bear thine eyes straight, though thy proud heart go wide.

Sonnet 140

The rejected lover, full of self-pity, begs the beloved not to press him too hard in her 'disdain' ~ he does not want to speak ill of her.

The curse of Venus

'Since thou art dead, lo, here I prophesy
Sorrow on love hereafter shall attend.
It shall be waited on with jealousy,
Find sweet beginning, but unsavoury end,
  Ne'er settled equally, but high or low,
  That all love's pleasure shall not match his woe.

'It shall be fickle, false and full of fraud,
Bud and be blasted in a breathing while,
The bottom poison, and the top o'erstrawed
With sweets that shall the truest sight beguile.
  The strongest body shall it make most weak,
  Strike the wise dumb, and teach the fool to speak.'

Extract from 'Venus and Adonis'

After the untimely death of Adonis, Venus places a curse on love and prophesies that it will bring nothing but conflict, destruction and misery.